MUSHROOM MARATHON
Running Toward the Prize of Serenity

By

Lynn Moriarty Parman

© 2004 by Lynn Moriarty Parman. All rights reserved.

No part of this book may be reproduced, stored in a retrieval system, or transmitted by any means, electronic, mechanical, photocopying, recording, or otherwise, without written permission from the author.

First published by AuthorHouse 09/18/04

ISBN: 1-4184-6370-1 (e-book)
ISBN: 1-4184-4285-2 (Paperback)

Library of Congress Control Number: 2002095188

This book is printed on acid free paper.

Printed in the United States of America
Bloomington, IN

Dedication: This book is dedicated to my parents who always encouraged their children's talents and gave me the most important gift of all…their faith in God, which helped me to overcome the obstacles that occurred during my race to serenity.

The following poem is a wonderful tribute to my parents.

VACATIONS ON THE FARM

My dear Auntie Max and dear Uncle "B"
I've come from California for your 50th Anniversary
You've both stood as one—thru thick and thru thin
And I'm grateful to God that you are my kin
Now raisin' five kids, I'm sure was a chore
But you always said "Why, there's room for one more"
So out from the city on vacations I'd come
To laugh, run and play 'neath the warm Iowa sun
From in-the-house to the outhouse and all 'round the farm
You know it's funny, but I never came to any harm
I'd go gather the eggs with Carol, my cousin
But the amount I'd collect was 12 shy of a dozen
For this city girl was afraid of the chickens
They pecked hands and legs; Gosh, it hurt like the dickens
If you'd been my real parent, you couldn't have done more
To make me feel welcome, much loved and cared for
I know that I speak for the folks here; and me
You're a shining example of how marriage should be
So dearest Auntie Max and you, too, Uncle "B"
I'll close this poem with hugs and kisses, all my best wishes
And "I promise tonight that I'll help with the dishes"
                                        Glenda Glee   1986

Note: Glenda died of cancer in July, 1996. She never lived to celebrate Mom and Dad's 60th Anniversary in September of that year. I miss her and I'm grateful for those childhood memories that we shared. I wish she were here to share the joy of seeing my first book in print.

TABLE OF CONTENTS

Part One–Short Essays

- TUNNEL OF DARKNESS 1
- MY HOLY PLACE 3
- THE PREGNANT CORNFIELD 5
- FLYING IN FORMATION 7
- ECHOS 9
- MENDING FENCES 11
- SORTIN' HOGS 13
- MY DOG SCOUT 15
- LONG LIVE THE FLAG 17
- LOOKIN' GOOD 19
- THE GREATEST FISHERMAN 21
- WILLINGNESS 23
- THE CODE OF THE COUNTRY 25
- THE VETERAN SURVIVES 27

Part Two–Poems and Inspiration

- CHRISTMAS AT OUR HOUSE 29
- CANOPY OF LOVE 31
- EGGS 33
- SWINGING BACK HOME 35
- OLD GARDNERS NEVER DIE 37
- THE CARNIVAL DOLL 39
- RIVER OF PEACE 41
- OLD VETERANS NEVER DIE 43
- A POT OF GOLD 45
- OH, GREAT SPIRIT 47
- THE LITTLEST WRANGLER 49
- THE LITTLEST PONY 51
- WALKING FOR THE WOUNDED 53
- THEY CALL HER GRAMMA 55
- THE CHILL IN THE AIR 57
- THE FARMERS SUPER BOWL 59
- DAVID'S GARDEN 61
- SEASONAL BEGINNINGS 63
- LIVING CLOSE TO NATURE 65
- BORN IN LOVE 67
- DUST MITE SAGA 69

Part Three–Longer Essays

- SATELLITE REFLECTIONS 71
- EMPTY POCKETS 73
- FLOODED CIRCUMSTANCES 75
- BARN RESTORATION 77
- THE WORLD'S GREATEST WATCH DOG 79
- SURROGATE MOTHER 81
- TAKING INVENTORY, WHAT'S IN THE FRUIT CELLAR? 83
- THE THONG TREE 85
- LETTER FROM TEDDY 87
- ONE LEG UP 89
- MUSHROOM MARATHON 91

INTRODUCTION

A marathon is an endurance contest…and someone wins the prize. This is a collection of reflections that have occurred since a 26-year marathon ended in recovery of my self-esteem. It is a second marriage (which happens to be to a farmer) that brings me back to nature and allows me to view past events in a much more spiritual light. Serenity becomes the prize to seek. And when you find it, your self-esteem is where it needs to be. You exhibit more self-confidence and trust in the Father of Creation.

People drop everything to search for the mighty morel when mushroom season arrives. However, we as hunters each have our own 'timing' for discovering that elusive prize of serenity in ourselves. A farm becomes My Holy Place and the marathon becomes a leisurely 'jog' after learning acceptance and thanksgiving. Appreciating life around me, indoors or out makes for a much less stressful existence.

My hope is that those who read *Mushroom Marathon* can also find the prize of peace in their own race to the finish line of true happiness.

TUNNEL OF DARKNESS

Today I was inspired by a mole. Not the brown spot on my skin, but a smooth little creature that has no eyes. He came out on top of the ground and burrowed all around my feet and the large rock I sat upon. I've felt like that sometimes—in the dark about where my life could be going. I would come out once in awhile to feel God's sun on my back. Sometimes a spiritual friend imparts that warmth to me. I had burrowed deep inside myself after the traumatic event of divorce from my alcoholic husband. I didn't trust anyone. I would go backwards in the tunnel of familiarity, clinging to old wounds. Like the mole is nourished by grubs in the ground, I too, feed spiritually when I am in darkness. I've sometimes regressed to old behaviors and had to admit my life was unmanageable again. Like the mole, I didn't know where I was going; but when I trusted God, a light pierced my blindness. God uses people and events as flashlights in my tunnel. When I trust Him, He gets me where He wants me to be—sometimes a light in someone else's tunnel of despair.

Lynn Moriarty Parman

MY HOLY PLACE

What's so special about the sights and sounds and smells of country living in the Midwest? Frustration with a computer job, had driven me often to make reservations at a rural retreat house, Wakonda (an Indian word meaning "Holy Place"). There, the ancient Indian tradition (nature) temporarily quiets my soul. It was there that I made one of the most important decisions of my life—to begin a second marriage—that would mean leaving family, friends, and job.

The winding hills of North Missouri are a welcome refuge from the rush to a job with no future. A secluded farmstead, the wooded pasture-lands and the low-hanging trees (like praying hands) over the river are a constant restoration for a once-disillusioned spirit.

The pungent smell of fresh hay is like a romp in the haymow of yesteryear when my brother and I built hay tunnels in the barn on a rainy day. The bellows of cattle in the early hours of dawn recall the barefoot girl in pigtails who rounded up the cows in the far pasture at milking time. The pure lilting song of a meadowlark perched on the top fence-wire in his black-breasted tuxedo, revives the feeling that I was attending a concert in a great auditorium during a leisurely walk to country school.

Daily chores have become a cultural event on dirt roads, under a canopy of trees that filters out the harsh rays of the summer sun and rests my eyes on my own private botanical garden, a profusion of wildflowers. They grow in any kind of soil reminding me that I can bloom wherever I put down roots.

A ripening field of wheat, moving in the soft breeze, resembles a prayer group, hands upraised, swaying to some heavenly melody beyond the range of my ears. They are all sizes, tall, average, and short—some straight, slightly bent, and skinny. Some full and fat. Various shades of color in different stages of ripening—like the peoples of the earth—reminding me of my purpose in God's plan, to live in harmony with all others.

It seems that the best has been saved for the autumn of my life. It's harvest time and blessings abound. My heart sings like the chorus of birds in the river's early morning mist. The summer's joy is intensified when a bluebird (symbol of happiness) nests in the old corner-post of the front yard. What a transcending experience moving to Missouri has been for me! A farm has become my Holy Place.

Lynn Moriarty Parman

THE PREGNANT CORNFIELD

Snuggled into the fertile womb of Mother Earth, little seeds, warmed by early season sun, germinate in moist surroundings. I think of that tiny speck of grain as an embryo, with cells dividing and quivering like a new butterfly emerging from the damp lining of a cocoon. The kernel bursts open extending long, slender leaves into it's environment. Those tender seedlings are nurtured by herbicides, insecticides, and fertilizers, the antibiotics and vitamins of the grain world.

A field of hybrid corn, like a waiting room of pregnant women has constant supervision. Safeguards may be utilized to guarantee a good harvest, but it's still subject to circumstances beyond the control of the most diligent specialist.

Delicate light leaves reach upwards for the clouds and by the fourth month, the tract is clothed in dark green with yellow plumage—standing at attention, like a co-ed drill team. The tall tassels, rustling like the silvery leaves of a cottonwood, begin to drop their golden bits of pollen on the fresh virgin silks of the young ears, impregnating the fruit of the womb. In the midst of that glorious surge of growth-the puberty of the corn cycle—disaster looms on the horizon.

Nature breathes a warning as dry Gulf Winds turn into a blowtorch leaving Grand Canyon cracks in the ground, like a ruptured placenta, draining life slowly away. Rare early morning dew resembles beads of perspiration while the plants attempt to utilize each drop of precious moisture.

The little kernels begin to swell like a batch of bread rising in the summer heat, but the midsummer drought threatens to abort the crop at several stages. After the field overcomes the odds of an unusually harsh season, then labor becomes imminent.

As the combine skillfully severs the umbilical cord to Mother Earth, the mound in the crib culminates delivery. Bulging bins, again, resemble pregnant women and the promise of a new generation.

Lynn Moriarty Parman

FLYING IN FORMATION

Hundreds of V's stretching from west to eastern horizons, like ribbons of black beads waving across the sky. V's within V's, hundreds of leaders all going the same Northwesterly direction, honking for others to follow. It's not just the flock that hears. Their calls echo down to the ground below.

Come! Let's fly together. Into the Northlands. Indian lore says "North" is the cold, dark times that come upon our lives. If we hang together we'll be ok. There is comfort and safety in being part of the flock. We don't need to go it alone. There will always be someone willing to make the journey by our side. Especially Jesus. We need never feel alone.

Did you know that when one goose falls out of formation, two more go with him to accompany him back to the flyway? And even if he isn't able to travel (he dies), there are still two left to travel together. Jesus can be that kind of partner. Geese mate for life. If we could have that kind of dedication to God, we would never "fall out of formation" without knowing there was someone to help us back in.

Lynn Moriarty Parman

ECHOS

HELLO, Hello, hello. Have you ever stood on a hill and yelled down into the valley? Your voice bounces from one hollow to another. Was it heard by anyone?

God gave his ten commandments, (engraved in stone) upon a mountaintop. His booming voice echoed with Moses back down into the valley. But when Moses got back, the people were already worshipping a golden calf.

Moses echoed God's words of the very first commandment, "I am the Lord your God, Thou shalt not have strange Gods before me!" Moses threw the tablets down in anger, breaking them in two.

We have continued breaking God's commandments ever since. Why isn't His voice heard and recognized in the valleys? Do I just look for mountaintop experiences? Do I even see God upon the peaks? Or am I worshipping "Self" when I accomplish some goal?

Don't we know that God is in each of us wanting to echo out into others lives? Like a pebble dropped in a pond creates ever widening circles? We never know how far an echo will carry. Something we do or say now may affect somebody, we do not even know, in a place we have never been, clear across the valley.

When I cupped my hands around my mouth and shouted "Hello-o-0-0," a beautiful doe came bounding out of the patch of timber. My voice had echoed back with a wonderful sight for my eyes to behold. She stood watching me, walked a few steps and seemed unafraid. Thank you Father for meeting me in this unexpected encounter, for reminding me that you do answer our prayers, sometimes softly, with a gift from nature.

Lynn Moriarty Parman

MENDING FENCES

Sometimes I want to sleep curled up in a fetal position...go back to the beginning...to the feeling of being safe and protected from the world, within the boundaries of my Mother's womb...but I couldn't stay there...life in the outside world is forced upon us and we learn...we either climb fences...or fall off of them. We tear them down...or build them higher as our response to each of life's sufferings. The pains of birth may be felt for a lifetime. I've come full circle, from being born on Grandma's farm to living on a farm in the evening of my life. As I accompany my husband to fix fences over the water gaps, I reflect on the twists and turns my own life took in the ditches or rolling pastures of the past.

Cutting a neighbor's bull out of our herd of heifers was as difficult as sorting the alcoholic out of my life after the decision was made to change some boundaries. The abusive relationship had trampled all the grass of self-respect between the fences, and I had to find "greener pastures" for my soul or die.

Wild deer cause a lot of damage to fences as they knock the staples loose during a mis-calculated flight from some real or imaginary foe. Those dangling wires remind me of the times I let my defenses down when some wild idea tripped across the boundaries of my field of vision.

I had to learn to say "NO" to some temptations and "YES" to some sufferings by bringing Jesus into the center of my pasture and making a permanent shrine for Him. I've learned that practicing forgiveness of my own and other people's selfishness is the only way to mend fences in relationships.

Lynn Moriarty Parman

SORTIN' HOGS

Sortin' hogs must be like God herding people toward the gate of heaven. Some pigs refused to cross a pen to get to the corral. There are those people today who likewise don't want to be corraled into a religion or a life-style they see as confining. There were three of us sortin' hogs... There are three of God: Father, Son and Spirit trying to herd His adopted children toward heaven's corral.

Sometimes our stubbornness earns us a sound whack on the nose or some other equally humbling chastisement. We get ourselves into deep, deep mud holes and God lets it happen until we finally see the gateway as the only way to go.

The first stubborn pig was allowed to go back to his old friends and old ways. He'll be dealt with later. When does a piglet become a hog? When he stubbornly bullies his way into the trough, making sure he consumes what he wants before any others have eaten? How many times are we allowed to 'go back' to the trough of drinking, drugs, or gambling, (many corruptible behaviors) to learn another lesson? Sometimes it takes many traumas of 'sortin' to be brought to our knees to follow the Master. Few of us are little lambs following the Shepherd for "many are called, but few are chosen."

Lynn Moriarty Parman

MY DOG SCOUT

A scout usually went ahead of the Wagon Train to see any signs of danger or to scout the best path for the wagons to take.

Our dog Scout runs ahead of us when we head out to the pasture. He thinks he knows where we are going. But after he's out of sight he forgets his goal. He wanders into a hay field following some interesting scent with his nose.

Do we sometimes try to go ahead of God, thinking we know His way? Then a temptation causes us to veer off in a different direction and forget the goal we set for ourselves, a goal we would have reached sooner if we had stayed with our Master along the way.

A guide is as good as his training has made him. When we've been over the road more than once, we have presumably learned the correct way and therefore can be qualified to lead others. Christ had as his guide, the Almighty Father in heaven. He knew instinctively what he had to do.

My dog Scout is filled with energy but it's often not channeled in the right direction. When we choose Jesus as our scout, we will never lose the way, for He will lead us to the eternal destination we are traveling toward, in a much more peaceful fashion. Although He never promised the road would be smooth, he did promise He would accompany us through every twist and turn, thereby making every road passable.

Lynn Moriarty Parman

LONG LIVE THE FLAG

D-Day...The troops have landed...under the banner of the American flag! It flies over the capital in Wash. D.C. watching the world's greatest leaders put their heads together. It flies to the aid of other countries who are in conflict. Now it flies free in the heartland of America, no smoke nor smog nor witnessing the violence between those it was meant to protect. Flying proudly, over the farmstead of one of it's veteran soldiers, the flag endures the wrath of tornado alley, whipping in retaliation for all the growing pains of her motherland.

Some days it hangs limp...absolutely no energy to wave. On those days, I wonder if she is ashamed of the troubles our nation has gotten itself into, ashamed of the waste at every level of government. Would our forefathers shudder at the ways their Bill of Rights are now being interpreted? Has 'Old Glory's reputation been tarnished?

The Grand Union Flag, first stitched by hand with needle and thread involving delicate stitches and great patriotic fervor, was born in 1775 when it first flew over the ships of The Colonial Fleet on the Delaware river. Long live the flag... May it always remain a symbol of the many nationalities that came together in Colonial America to draft the constitution for a brand new nation. May it never have to experience its own D-Day, the death of the principles that conceived it.

Lynn Moriarty Parman

LOOKIN' GOOD

Men are predominantly visually oriented: they notice the physical. Instead of saying "Thanks for helping this morning," he says "You're an awful good-lookin' woman." The definition of "awful" is bad, dreadful, terrible, horrible, etc, or awe-inspiring, awesome, wondrous, solemn, amazing etc. He gets great pleasure because she fixes her hair, whether they are going somewhere or just sortin' hogs at 7:30 in the morning.

She quietly smiles back at him and is amused by his choice of words. It's easy to tell when they're being appreciative, no matter what words are used. Since he knows her equally as well, her moods, etc., she believes he sees more in her than just her hair.

She thinks she must be "lookin' good" to him because he sees her willingness to help cheerfully, whenever they need another hand to move equipment or sort livestock. Serving the Father through daily interruptions and sometimes the chaos of equipment breakdowns can be a great opportunity to practice patience. Could the vision mirrored in hubby's eyes really be a reflection of her faithfulness to her God?

She hopes the second definition of awful is what he sees.

Lynn Moriarty Parman

THE GREATEST FISHERMAN

God is the greatest fisherman. He can dangle the bait of eternal bliss right in front of me, and I still think worldly catches look more appealing. He made the sea and he stocked it with many different species (races). But people didn't get along very good, killing each other, refusing to follow ten simple commandments. However, God has enormous patience.

He waits for me to grab his bait and follow Him, hook, line and sinker. The only problem is, the hook is invisible. I can't even see the bait when it's right under my nose. And once I'm caught I have to make the choice of whether to stay on the line. You're always free to go.

What if I do make the right choice? Then I may experience the proverbial "fish bowl" syndrome. Others will look and watch my behavior. "Has she really changed since she 'got religion?'" I must ask myself, "Have I really given up foraging selfishly at the bottom of the sea?"

Jesus said, "Be fishers of men" to the apostles. When we are caught in the net of christianity it means we start fishing for Jesus' love to draw others closer to God. We become the bait, like a neon lure, that God dangles in front of another trophy for his kingdom. How elated the Father must be when an unsuspecting soul is snagged for his banquet in heaven, or how excited when he sees us actually fishing for His Son's love?

Whether I have dived too deep into life's pressure chamber or sailed over the waves of tranquility, it's as if the sea-world were a giant eye-ball. I cannot escape God's gaze no matter where I go. If God doesn't catch me in my lifetime, I may never see his heavenly aquarium. I will then be judged for how I took the bait, whether I ran with it or just completely ignored it.

And what if I were caught, then broke the line by swimming forcefully away in another direction? Chances are that the next time I take the bait, I will be a much bigger trophy because I have suffered for my arrogance and I will be more inclined towards repentance.

Are you willing to humbly take the bait and swim wherever God leads you? Yes, to become a student of his own "school" where he can teach you all you need to know from the Bible, the textbook of the Greatest Fisherman on earth!

Lynn Moriarty Parman

Willingness

One cow had twins. Another lost her calf so they put one twin with that cow. The farmer put a patch of fur from the dead calf on the back of the new calf and hoped the cow would accept it as her own. She would not, and kicked it across the stall. The little calf faced rejection but kept trying to nurse—she was hungry. After a week the cow still kicked when the calf tried to nurse, so the farmer kept tying her up three times a day to let the calf get fed.

I observed the cow's unwillingness to accept a new idea. How much do we fight it in our own lives? Don't let anyone get too close—they might hurt you. That cow was grieving her lost baby. She was reluctant to share herself with another one. How many innocent "calves" does God put before us to coerce us into acceptance of our circumstances? How many times do we reject the people or incidents he sends us while trying to teach us obedience and humility? The calf nuzzles the cow's nose, but is still kicked away from the dinner table. We may tolerate ideas briefly, but fight total acceptance. It takes willingness to strive for acceptance.

Finally, while the cow was eating grain, she became willing to let the calf nurse. Sometimes we are more willing while we are pre-occupied with something else. The cow accepted the calf, then her whole attitude changed as she became defensive, even to protecting her 'baby.' We must be willing to accept changes whole-heartedly then defend our principles as the best way to encourage others to change.

Lynn Moriarty Parman

THE CODE OF THE COUNTRY

In the country it is customary to feed whoever happens to be working on the premises at noon. I even fed the furnace repair men once. The unwritten Code of the Country is changing as people distance themselves from each other. There seems to be an 'I don't care' attitude that prevails everywhere. Where is Christ's biblical example to serve others?

Jesus fed the multitude without deciding that this one or that one was more deserving. He fed them all. We today are selective. The code of the country prevailed because people read the Bible and tried to follow it's precepts in their everyday lives. People were kinder to each other because they were in tune with God's Word. And if we aren't kind to those close to us, how can we see the need of others?

We are to seek Christ's face in the hungry, the homeless, the imprisoned, the sick. Well, maybe the hungry is your neighbor helping to do your chores. We don't have to go to Africa to find the hungry. It is our attitude right here in our neighborhood that is so important. So often the hungry aren't hungry for food but hungry for love and kindness. Some are the imprisoned, held captive by emotional pain inflicted upon them as children.

We can do more evangelizing through our kindness to the neighbors than all the 'preaching' in the world. How many "neighbors" do we really have? We drive by their house every day and never stop to say "How are you?" For if we did, we might somehow become involved. We keep our distance...if we get too close they might treat us badly! So I'll ignore them first before they have a chance to ignore me!

Christ never ignored anyone! He saw the tax collector who climbed the tree to get a glimpse of him, the woman who touched his cloak in the crowd, the beggar beside the pool. He was always in tune with those around him. The woman at the well by custom was not supposed to speak to men. But he told her all the things she'd done and she learned from him. Will Christ also tell us everything we ever did? If we wait till we die, we won't have much chance to change. But if we seek Christ in our neighbor etc., gradually we become conscious of our own sins of omission. We become aware of negative attitudes and want to change. We'll become hungry for God's grace. And when the neighbors treat us badly, the old code of the country (the Good Book) must prevail.

Lynn Moriarty Parman

THE VETERAN SURVIVES

Recently our state permitted Combat Infantry liscence plates for Korean War Veterans. My husband proudly ordered one for our car. One day early in March it was snowing all afternoon. The gravel roads were getting slick. A car was coming over the next hill, so I touched my brakes to pull along the side to wait for it to pass. My car promptly began fish tailing. Defensive steering did not help...it was out of control, all over the country road...and going down hill.

All I could think of was the deep ditch at the bottom of the hill. My car miraculously headed for the bank on the left of the road, stopped with a jolt, swinging the back end around to crash into the same bank. I was somewhat shaken by the what if's. But since I had front-wheel drive, I wondered...... "Could I drive out (up hill)?" I was surprised! It worked and I headed back home, too scared to even report the incident.

Later I looked at the front of the car. The liscense plate was gone, the plastic frame all torn up and grass hanging from the whole bumper. I couldn't see any other damage but knew I had to tell—because 4-8 inches of new snow was in that evening's forecast.

I got up the courage to report to "headquarters" and he just about declared war! Instead he drove me over to the battle site in the pickup. There it was, the Combat Infantry Badge "plate" standing on end in the snow bank, like a rifle and bayonet holding a helmet for a casualty. But like my husband, who survived the battle at Massacre Valley in Feb. 1951, his liscense plate survived and could be bent back into shape. It too is now a Veteran—of a winter snowstorm in '95.

Lynn Moriarty Parman

Mushroom Marathon
Running Toward the Prize of Serenity

CHRISTMAS AT OUR HOUSE

It was Christmas Eve and all through the house
Everyone slept except Mom and her spouse

The stockings were hung by the tree with great care
But after Midnight Mass, underneath was still bare

The kids were asleep, all warm in their beds
While dreams of Santa Claus raced through their heads

Mom in her nightgown, Dad too, undressed
They just settled down for a short little rest

When beside the bed there rang a loud noise
And Mother got up to unpack the toys

The closet was hiding each ones present
While the moon shone full, not just a crescent

One moment later, there sounded a noise
Could it be the girls?...Nope,...one of the boys!

It came from the stairway, steps did creak
Was someone wise and gonna' peak?

Mama hesitated near the living room couch
While on the stairs, did David slouch?

Steps creaked again, then Mom arose
Crossed to the stairs, saw ten pink toes

Lynn Moriarty Parman

It was David, all right, now sitting real still
Waiting for Santa, with a great big thrill

Mother said "Get yourself to bed
Or Santa won't come to you, sleepyhead"

He knew what that meant, not even one toy...
So he scampered to bed like a good little boy.

Then Mom began sorting things out,
That she was excited, there was no doubt.

When each surprise around the tree was placed
With five name tags, back to bed she paced.

Anxious to please, deep in thought
Hoping the kids liked what they got.

Kids hadn't guessed Dad in a Santa suit
At the one room school, in his old red boot

'Twas worth a million to hear their applause
Before they knew the real Santa Claus

Who in secret planned to make Christmas gay
But believed Christ's birth, the most joyous way!

1953

CANOPY OF LOVE

Heavenly Father, I see a road on a hill over there, emerging on the other side of the forest and I see my life. I have to get through the trees to find the path on the other side. Will I ever get out of these woods? It seems one trauma after another comes at me and some days I can't even see daylight. Remind me Lord, that your love is like those branches above, an umbrella, keeping me safe from the storm going on around me. Thank you, O Father for being with me in the forest.

1986

Lynn Moriarty Parman

EGGS

Good Eggs get lots of praise
All their life through

Bad Eggs try hard to reverse
An image sometimes untrue.

Some save Nest Eggs for
A special dream they hold

Someone else just laid on Egg
An idea not so bold.

You're an eggs-ceedingly Good Egg. I have eggs-amined past eggs-perience And I'm eggs-hilarated that you have been a good eggs-ample. Humpty Dumpty fell off the wall and eggs-ploded. I am Handled with Care. I am eggs-cited to eggs-press eggs-actly how I feel. I eggs-ercise my right to say, "I am a Good Egg because of you."

Lynn Moriarty Parman

SWINGING BACK HOME

*Perpetual kids go flying
Up, up in the air so high
IN Grandpa and Gramma's tree
We all give a great big sigh.*

*Swinging back through our childhood
We're lost in the clouds of time
Where soda pop, now 60 cents
Used to be just a dime*

*The tree we liked to climb
Where sweet daydreams lingered hours
Like a pretty butterfly
Among the fragrant flowers.*

*Oh, to be that joyful now
Swinging one day to another
Who was it fostered "wonder"?
God blessed our Dad & Mother!*

Lynn Moriarty Parman

OLD GARDNERS NEVER DIE

Old gardeners never die
They plant connecting bonds
Garden Club memories
Like gold reflections on ponds

Flower Show schedules
Environmental Care
Horticulture study
Every member was there

Some held local office
Once or even twice
For some—group organizing
Meant days with extra spice

Planting trees, clean-up days
Or weeding with a hoe
Bake sale or county fair
They worked like an old "pro"

Dividing perennials
Spread blossoms of joy
Seedlings, slips or cuttings
Were like a shared toy

Lynn Moriarty Parman

*Tulip Festival fun
Or educational tours
But inspiration shared
Sowed the seed that endures*

*Old gardeners never die
Their friendship lingers on
Lizzie, Marcella, Marge or Feryl
Can't today, put their fingers on*

*But their words of wisdom
Have crept into our creed
For old gardeners never die
They might just go to seed*

*And grow a golden memory
That years will never dim
For God gave old gardeners
A gift-the reflection of HIM.*

Mushroom Marathon
Running Toward the Prize of Serenity

THE CARNIVAL DOLL

Screams of laughter and sometimes fear
From carnival rides of yesteryear
Sideshow barkers entice the curious
Summer magic made girls delirious

Toss a ring, throw a penny, pound the maul
Win a big teddy bear or a painted doll
Grandmother's eyes were bright with joy
To behold her "double" as a new toy

After many years, that doll is restored
A granddaughter, misty dreams will horde
Upon Sally's shelf, this princess will reign
Bringing delight to a young girls' eye again.

Lynn Moriarty Parman

RIVER OF PEACE

Along my river of life, the current represents the world...Heavenly Father, it's too easy to go along with worldly ways...... I am disturbed by anger today. It's so hard to hold my tongue, but I know things will accelerate if I don't..........I'll just sit here on the river bank for awhile..........I know why I just cut my finger when I was cutting bittersweet vines...the anger had control of me............ A soft breeze is blowing the leaves on the water UPSTREAM. Let the gentle breath of the Spirit carry me against the world.......Praise you Jesus, you are my peace.

Lynn Moriarty Parman

OLD VETERANS NEVER DIE

Old veterans never die
They just stick by their guns
Especially when today's mail
Brings a stack of duns

Principles seem simple
When patriotism runs deep
If war duty calls, young men
Scramble upon a jeep

When command orders mean
They'll be shipping overseas
They follow Uncle Sam's ideals
Often, down upon their knees

England, France, Japan by ship
Korea or Viet Nam
Purple Hearts, Medals of Honor
From shrapnel, shells or bomb

Army, Navy, Air Corps, Marine
Survival, the moment's game
If they get back home alive
That might be their claim to fame

Lynn Moriarty Parman

*Soldiers serve society
With every occupation
While hearts contain a certain pride
Protecting this greater nation*

*Years roll on—cadence dims
Parasites or Agent Orange,
Battle fatigue or malaria...breed
Some illnesses strange*

*Old vets benefits questioned
Not all can call on their nurses
From those who haven't privilege
You might hear a soldier's curses*

*AIDS fears or homelessness
In America, foreign battles rage
The turn of the century holds a deficit
As we turn the history page*

*Old veterans never die
They fight 'till they can't run
And when the great Commander calls
Trade final victory for their gun.*

A POT OF GOLD

The hills of North Missouri
As green as 'County Kerry'
Where leprechauns are dancing
To ballads of the prairie

Where Irishmen have traveled
And one fair lass calls home
Who has found her 'pot of gold'
In the woods, where she can roam

Lynn Moriarty Parman

OH, GREAT SPIRIT

Oh, Great Spirit, you have helped me face the cold winds of the North, giving me strength and endurance. Hurts were overcome.

Your Spirit came out of the East, making me yearn for the sunrise and a new day. You planted the gift of sorrow in my heart, and a determination to keep 'starting over.'

And when the South winds blow, I am comforted when I'm tired. You have warmed me with a desire to stay close to you. You are the hearth that is home.

Now during the aging process, I am facing West, the direction where the sun goes down. Help me to keep my faith glowing in beautiful colors as I come to greet you.

You have nurtured me with food from the Earth and your Spirit from the Air. Thank you for caring for me so completely, for being my Creator. Let all of Nature lift my mind to you so that I will always accept your truth. Amen.

Lynn Moriarty Parman

THE LITTLEST WRANGLER

Heigh-ho, heigh-ho
Off to Grandpa's farm I go

To wear my cowboy jeans
To eat cornbread and beans

I'll ride on Grandpa's horse
And then go fishing, of course

Ride the swing, real high or low
And romp and play in a green meadow

The littlest wrangler, a good little boy
Already has a tractor toy

Grandpa's house is not the same
Since the "littlest wrangler" came!

Lynn Moriarty Parman

Mushroom Marathon
Running Toward the Prize of Serenity

THE LITTLEST PONY

The littlest wrangler has a need
For a pony or racing steed
To go fishing in summer's heat
To sit high in the saddle seat
To help Grandpa fix a fence
Or ride off to the timber dense
To take off on a fast gallop
Or reach down to pull a pal up
To hold onto the reins
Like every boy from the plains
We give him the Littlest Pony
And his name is "Macaroni"

Lynn Moriarty Parman

WALKING FOR THE WOUNDED

Emotionally
Physically wounded
Wheel chair bound
I walked
For you today
And prayed each step
That touched the ground.
Thanked our dearest
Lord
For you I've found
Who gives me reason
HIS door to hound.
I walked for you today
You heard not one
Small sound.
I thanked HIM for
Your smile
That never ceases
To astound.
Yesterday I walked
Wounded around
Imprisoned by pain
Mushroomed
Into a mound.
Today I walked
For you
My stride would
Pound ... unto me a
Grateful heart
While pity HE
unwound.

Lynn Moriarty Parman

Mushroom Marathon
Running Toward the Prize of Serenity

THEY CALL HER GRAMMA

Nothing on earth annoys
Grand little girls or grand little boys
When Gramma's making more stuffed toys!

Pink elephants, ponies or clowns
Sleeping bags or flannel nightgowns
And traveling to more distant towns

100 or 200 long cheerful miles
To see her grand-kid's great smiles
And share in triumphs or trials

Warm hugs mean so very much
From kids, whether Irish or Dutch
But "I love you Gramma"—the greatest touch

Sometimes she sends things by mail
Brithdays and Christmas 'without fail'
Five days...seems like 'the Overland Trail'

They say "Gramma, can we come to the farm?"
Who can resist grandchildren's charm?
Her heart melts, "I see no harm!"

Lynn Moriarty Parman

*They call her Gramma so sweet
Even when they come trick-or-treat
When Gramma got "Great"—that was neat*

*She wondered "How can I be great?"
Not just doing the fishing bait
But listening to hearts describing a date?*

*So when she's older and travels not
Knocks on her door will mean a lot
'Cause grandkids bring their own little tot*

*Letters of love are more labored now
And there's no more reunion pow-wow
Ears and joints don't work anyhow*

*"Gramma" means infinite love
God sprinkles His grace from above
No one would flaunt a white glove*

*Because 'Gramma' chose the better part
Nurturing a little one's heart
The housework? Tomorrow she'll start*

Mushroom Marathon
Running Toward the Prize of Serenity

THE CHILL IN THE AIR

Autumn's chill is in the air
And leaves piled in the streets
As the city commanded

Friends K.J. and Nicholas…
Laughing, dive under a mound
Next to the curb, they've landed

Hiding beneath, they listen
To the crackling and rustling
Like a bowl of cornflakes expanded

What's that revving sound?
A teen thinks leaf piles are fun,
He's swerving his truck, single-handed

Mothers become frantic
Combing their neighborhood
Where could these kids be stranded?

An hysterical mom finds her son
But he doesn't hear her scream—
Too late to be reprimanded

A deadly chill descends on the air
Over two young hockey players
Heavenly angels have banded

Who can understand
Or trust what God
In his wisdom commanded?

"Let the children come
to me, for heaven belongs
to these." They're branded.

Lynn Moriarty Parman

Mushroom Marathon
Running Toward the Prize of Serenity

THE FARMERS SUPER BOWL

Robins on the fencepost
Woodpecker pounds a new hole
Earthworms leaving trails
While the mare feeds her new foal

Grass is getting greener
Little league dreams of bases stole
Doggie drags stuff by the yard
Mother Nature's in her second quarter goal

The river doesn't flood this year
Wild turkeys are out on patrol
Corn planter's ready, no penalty here
Who will bet on the farmer's super bowl?

Lynn Moriarty Parman

DAVID'S GARDEN

Adam lived in a garden
Was forbid the fruit of one tree
Then Jesus prayed in a Garden
"Will you wait one hour with me?"

HE promised a better paradise
"Today you will be with me" to a thief
We must endure earth's troubles
To get any heavenly relief

David too had a garden
He tended the orchard trees
His lovely little "park"
Offered solitude and peace

Affliction opened the garden gate
Brain tumors made a painful demand
David came home to his "garden"
But took the path to God's holyland

Lynn Moriarty Parman

SEASONAL BEGINNINGS

Summer found a new beginning
When lovers pledged a vow
To love and trust each the other
Leaving "old" behind, new union now

Fall may burst the flowers' seed pod
But Love matures through seasons many
Watered deeply with the WORD
God should be the lucky penny

The husband—head of the house
As Jesus is head of his church
Walk in His ways, commandments ten
And His Spirit, you'll not besmirch

For all who obey and serve him
Have prosperity and pleasures
Patience, when conflicts arise
Serenity, one of the treasures

To be married in a later season
The bulb of love takes root
Fertilized by past years' wisdom
Happiness grows foot by foot

Lynn Moriarty Parman

Living Close to Nature

We don't have a log cabin
Or a camp in the woods
But Nature's at the back door
By insistent interludes
Whether it's June bugs a flyin'
I even found one in my bed!
Or mice in the attic
Chewing at a ceiling overhead
We're always plugging holes
So we won't be invaded
Yet Nature had her way
And the crickets serenaded!
I hear the wrens a singing
And it's music to my ears
But mosquitos in the house
Are buzzing bombadiers
Creatures prefer the earth
And my basement's another world
A three foot snake
Under the stairs, unfurled!
No crack is too small
For fugitives of Nature
They break every boundary
And rules of the legislature
Was that a cockroach
Under the kitchen sink?
Well, fix 'em a beer trap
Their tastes will become extinct
Ants on the kitchen floor
Have made a hiking trail
While they're on the march
I'm plotting how to assail
Just when all's under control
What's hopping across the room?
Why, it's a little green tree frog
Another country heirloom!
Will there ever be immunity
From a Mother Nature's member?
Nope...God's creatures are with us
From January to December!

Lynn Moriarty Parman

BORN IN LOVE

Born at birth or born at conception?
When was I really "born?"
God made me in my mother's womb.
Between these perceptions, I'm torn.

Is that my birthday in the February cold
Or is it really in the springtime of May?
For that's when God conceived a little girl
Choosing my mother…His Love to convey

I will live "as if" each birthday of mine
Is the day of a spring season's change
For that day was a whole new beginning
when the seed became "life," as God did arrange

I praise Him for the gift of my life
But the Gospel says "ye must be born again?"
If I'd seen Christ from my beginning
He wouldn't have to say "where have you been?"

For 'being born' is seeing greatness of the Lord
Few know it from the start.
Why must I seach a whole lifetime
For the Father's love…that was created in my heart?

Lynn Moriarty Parman

DUST MITE SAGA

Some ancestors used to bed down with the critters,
While even little "dust mites" give me the jitters!

How could anything so tiny you can't see,
Make my nose stuffy by sleeping with me?

Millions defecating upon my pillow...they say.
Is my bed a latrine or the ground where they play?

If the air is so foul, I can't breathe in my bedding,
Where do you think my health could be heading?

Our Mothers told jokes about little "dust bunnies"
Until a magnifying glass turned them into monies.

Such an ugly critter...shacked up in my hair!
If I change my bed daily, do you suppose they're still there?

I shower every night...which grandma couldn't do,
And the dryer whisks off lint, so no crud can accrue.

What I want to know is...when did they get started?
And what do they eat...for so much "stuff" discarded?

They say mites cause illness or allergies from infestation.
Would it be so, if we weren't creatures of co-habitation?

Two people lose more skin cells in one nights' slumber,
More fresh food for the mite colony...what a bummer!

My dead cells feeding another kind of creature,
While I'm the lead actor in my dream's double feature!

Now the ads in catalogs, try to make us aware.
Just buy sprays and special bedding...mites haven't a prayer!

Is there a chance the dust mite could become extinct?
The EPA would make them an endangered specie...methink.

Lynn Moriarty Parman

SATELLITE REFLECTIONS

Are you tuned in? Are your receptors turned on? My eyes and ears are miniature satellites absorbing signals from the heavens. God may be sending me a message in a sunset or in a movie on TV. It might come through a friend's voice or the sound of a soft rain. My 'dish' catches an abundance of God's grace when I concentrate on Him, especially with Christian broadcasts.

Like the robin perched amidst a flock of ordinary blackbirds on the light wires, my life can sing a song of praise. "Do not model yourselves on the behavior of the world, but let your behavior change, modeled by your new mind." (Rom. 12:2)

I must get rid of the ground clutter in order to zero in on God's signal meant for me. Distractions, like the wrong kinds of TV programs or acquaintances, often keep me from receiving a clear signal. "Do you not yet understand? Have you no perception? Are your minds closed?" (Mark 7:18, 19) When I focus on Jesus, he helps me tune out other distractions. He becomes my spiritual hearing aid to distinguish his Word in the gospel.

Sometimes I pay for the type of programming I select. In choosing a bad relationship, the price is lived out in emotional pain and crippled spirituality. I have been guilty of putting someone else before God.

When moving away from family and friends, loneliness encouraged me to pray for a Spiritual friend who would be on my wave-length. I met a lady, who had also been praying for a new friend after the death of her husband. The similarities in our lives were astonishing: same birth month; same hobbies and interests, even both of us had scarlet fever as children.

Although we had different church backgrounds and two generations of age between us, we shared a common love of Jesus. At times we called each other, not knowing that the other needed a listening ear, but the Master Program Director knew!

Reading the Bible every day is what we call fine-tuning our wave-length. The Universe is crowded with radio signals. What type of recurring feed are we allowing to enter our satellite system? We must hear the Word of God and live accordingly. "Blessed are those who hear the word of God and keep it." (Luke 11:27)

There are no installation charges when we choose to get on God's satellite. We already possess the equipment to tune into the Master's channel. Do we appreciate God's timing in our area of need? Yes, He knows the needs of his children. My new friend and I believed that He answered our simultaneous prayer...because we were listening.

Lynn Moriarty Parman

EMPTY POCKETS

"What's in your pocket?" "I have a pocketful of change." "Did you empty your pockets?" You never know what will surface in the laundry tub from a corner of someone's pocket. "Look, there's a dollar bill! "What's that log, bouncing around the whirlpool?"

Pockets are an everyday subject of conversation. There are the pockets of Pelicans, who use their bills to carry fish back to their young and squirrels who carry nuts in their cheeks to a safe storage place. How about the built-in nursery in a kangaroo pouch or the valuable resource discovered in a pocket of natural gas or oil? Those pockets have a practical purpose, but pockets on clothes fashions can be either serviceable or just plain decorative.

I can't turn my pockets inside out to empty them and they surely aren't a decoration because they are hidden, <u>high</u> and <u>low</u>, inside the garment of my skin. With a <u>Hi</u>-atal hernia at the bottom of the esophagus; everything that's eaten slides by this pocket, sometimes filled with bitter stomach acid and often causing great distress. It may erupt suddenly (which embarrasses me), sending belches up the chute or worse yet, offends with bad breath.

Several hours later, the garbage left from food processing passes through the lower colon. There again, it encounters more pockets, diverticu-<u>LO</u>-sis, that are like chuckholes in a neglected city street. Debris, such as small seeds, nuts or popcorn hulls fall off the load of garbage pushing by and can't get back on.

Gorging myself on peanuts was an abrasive that scraped the rim of the pocket, oozing out red blood like melted crayon. Any inflammation pulls on the emergency cord of eating habits to put the brakes on my nibbling tendencies.

I must sort food carefully because my pockets are traps, not treasures. Maintaining a vigilance over provisions, means that some things, (like delicate laundry), never find their way to the tub. Instead they require hand care; avoiding popcorn hulls and nuts, straining tomato seeds or buying seedless grapes for the low pocket—avoiding caffein, alcohol and spicy foods for the high one.

Unlike the laundry surprises which can be double-checked if tossed down the chute carelessly, or removed through a lid later; there is no fishing out bad choices once the edibles are agitated. Melted crayons add their own bit of artistry to the laundry cycle but food that looked so good before it was injested might also be a short-lived pleasure later.

Others may be responsible for feeding the laundry pile, but I am the only one depositing things in my mouth. Instead of putting myself through the wringer of diverticulitis or acid reflux, I choose to "handle with care" some of my favorite foods. So while I'm hanging out today's laundry, I feel like singing! "Hurray for empty pockets!!!!!!"

Lynn Moriarty Parman

FLOODED CIRCUMSTANCES

"I do set my bow in the cloud, and it shall be for a token of a covenant between Me and the earth." Gen. 9:13 The flood kept coming in '93. Why doesn't he spare me, spare my land? Was I only trusting feelings? They were pretty low as we dumped the rain guage every few days. 29 inches in the month of July!

I could be overwhelmed at the magnitude of the thing that dominated our summer, keeping us from getting the hay cut, drowning over 200 acres of crops and contaminating our well water. Feeding the pigs was like literally wallering in a pig sty. The poor animals used up all of their energy just climbing up out of the mud onto the cement feeding platform. And the day we had to pull four, 250 lb. hogs through the mud (to dispose of them) seemed a dark day indeed. Where was the sunshine the day my foot slipped off the feeding station and sank into slop over my knee-high boots? Tears went unnoticed, added to the rain drops already dripping off my brow.

A 500 lb. calf died of pneumonia, the damp air hindering his recovery. After livestock chores, the basement had to be pumped out. Furniture was piled at the high end of the hobby room and the carpet rolled up over it. Then my "Rainbow" vacuum came to the rescue as I spent hours in rubber boots sucking up the water that ran in a steady stream from walls and seams around the floor. I even contemplated drilling a hole in the floor (over the drain that ran underneath) because levees around the shower drain kept the water from draining away. And we lived on the hill, a distance above the river!

Twice a day was milking time for our Jersey cow and the mud on her udder meant an extra chore. The pond in her pasture completely disappeared under flood waters, not even a fence post visible. But that cow was the relief valve my husband needed from the terrible stress. He enjoyed that chore and could relax while milking the old-fashioned way.

Yet...there were mornings when the sun came up...even if for only a few minutes before more clouds loomed over the horizon. I found myself looking forward to that glimmer of sunlight and gazing at some absolutely breath-taking sunrises. That is meditation time. Often that sliver of sun was the "Amen" to an otherwise faltering prayer.

I captured on film one rainbow that seemed anchored in our river bed to the east with the other end raining it's misty energy into the big pond to the south. It felt like a miracle. God did indeed have us under the arch of his protection even in the midst of the summer deluge.

At the height of the flood, there was even a full moon that granted at least one evening of reprieve, reflecting romantically on the the lake that our "Grand" River had become. It was hard to imagine that the same tributary three years ago had been completely dry and we had walked across it (at the rainbow's end).

Agriculturalists tell us that soil can be killed, but may be brought back into production with long-term care. When our hopes and dreams for the material blessings of our land have been wrecked, we still have hope because the rainbow of God's covenant is a sure sign that nothing here matters anyway. If some are driven off the land by the flood, God's rainbow follows them to new situations. Oh, the clouds will surely come again and it may seem like there is no sun, but the SON is ALWAYS shining even when we are at our "flooded" place beneath the mire of unfavorable circumstances.

Tiny little hummingbirds were at their dining perch as early as daybreak, fluttering against the raindrops. They were the orchestra of gladness that punctuated my sliver of daily spiritual encounter.

July 21. Three hummingbirds! The new one is arrogant and proud, dressed in irridescent green with red scarf at his throat. He perches on a tomato cage and chases off each one that comes to the feeder. He is beautiful, but his attitude is less than charitable. He keeps up his game, chasing others away from the "table." A new player enters the game! A lowly sparrow begins chasing the proud one! The one who only has a bad reputation does a good deed.

I saw this same play being acted out by the celebrities and corporate officials who showed up on the sand-bagging operations along the hundreds of miles of threatened levees. Convicted prisoners filling sandbags alongside humble Amish and ministers of churches from far and near. Nothing else mattered but working toward a common goal, that of saving a town, or a water plant or thousands of acres of crops. In the end, despair seemed to win temporarily as levees burst, but the common faith of the people triumphed. All these other things will pass away...but His words shall not pass away. "What you do for my brother, you do for me." Matt. 25:40.

July 23...Two hummers at the feeder. What a blend of harmony to hear the whir of tiny wings while the roll of distant thunder put percussion to their song. The outdoor symphony begins at day break, playing intermittently until darkness once again descends.

Raging waters, irrespective of even the dead, washed most of a cemetery away. Bones gathered into a common grave were attributed the reverence felt appropriate. It's the living that are more easily disturbed. Seeing coffins out of their designated places, brings a feeling of irreverence.

Interestingly, if we try to bury an emotion, it won't stay buried. It comes to the surface again and again, until we honestly look at the resurrected anger, shame, pride, etc. and attempt to see what old patterns of behavior still affect us today. We will never be "at peace" until the remains of damaged emotions are gathered up and prepared for a proper burial. "Yea, though I walk through the valley of the shadow of death, I will fear no evil: for thou art with me; thy rod and thy staff they comfort me." PS 23:4 KJV

BARN RESTORATION

Her soul resembles a big majestic old barn, built upon a solid foundation of rock but surrounded by an aura of conscience, that inate knowledge of right and wrong. Sin begins as a mere suggestion in the mind. Worldly temptations begin subtley...first a hinge comes loose on the barn door at the lower level. It sags and lets in other temptations until the door falls completely off from overuse, (and neglect of repair).

Once temptations get past the first stall, they take up residence easily (like Barn Swallows). They become a nuisance, flying in and out at will. The more that people tolerate a nuisance, the more their defenses are let down. Soon they begin to think it won't hurt anything to let that desirous thought live in it's own corner of the hayloft.

The old barn becomes weakened by leaning towards the things of the WORLD, and begins to slip off it's foundation. The lightening rod on the roof no longer points straight up towards heaven. Most troublesome thoughts become like a rebel horse, raring up or kicking a board out of the side of the barn, not wanting to be restrained by a bit in it's mouth or tied to the post of anybody's conscience.

The once proud interior of the barn is now dirty from nests of rebellion built in it's rafters. The swallows of indecency have left droppings of guilt in every corner while the cobwebs of denial, obscure the sinner's vision.

An arrogant "cowboy" came riding down the highway when the barn owner was most vulnerable after divorce. He first called on the 2-way, getting his foot in the barn door when it was not latched. A cup of coffee seemed harmless enough...before she knew it, three hours had passed. His language seemed vulgar but that warning did not register. He began dismounting regularly at her hitching post and kept pestering her until he was invited to her house, even met her teenage son. The stranger was on ally when her son was admitted into drug treatment. She only needed someone to hold her hand and comfort her.

He even wanted to go to church with her one Sunday. They went...but she dragged a horrible headache along while ignoring that painful warning about her behavior. She wanted to believe that he meant it when he said he could fix things around her house, and looked at him as some kind of savior that could "fix" her poverty line existence. Minimum wages kept her in need and he gave her money. He was very knowledgeable of the Bible and knew just the right gait at which to run with her.

But the "cowboy" wasn't the only horse in the barn! There were two other decent male friends who took her out to eat regularly. Her mind got distracted at work trying to "juggle" the invitations around knowing when the "cowboy" would return. It was inevitable that she would get caught. She was a people-pleaser trying to be what each wanted, while all thought she was a good, honest woman.

When two of them butted heads at her stable, she knew she had to let the "cowboy" go. He was asking to bring his kids from another state to live with her. She didn't really know this guy. That was the reality that shocked her into refusing to let him darken her doorway again. She finally could choose good...over not good. The other two were still grazing near the barn, however.

All of this time that her barn doors needed repair, she was involved in a prayer group and Bible study. Self-esteem grew very, very slowly. The restoration work had begun on her conscience however, but until self-awareness grew enough, she could not make many good decisions about her life. One by one, she let go of the other two needy relationships. One had given her a bottle of TABU perfume, which most aptly described that relationship. Sinners subconsciously do know the truth, just can't face it honestly. The other friendship truly had trusted her and might have married her, had she listened and acted on the not so subtle hints.

Little by little, the lightening rod of God's love struck the roof, sending bolts of the Spirit's strength down to the lower level, straightening up the whole structure. The barn is lifted back on it's foundation of faith, the cobwebs of denial have disappeared, the nests of rebellion have been knocked down, the hay dust of the past has finally settled, letting the light of spiritual renewal radiate out through all of the windows.

Does this make the old restored barn eligible for the National Historic Register? She wouldn't apply for that kind of distinction. The only honor that really counted was the restoration of a weakened conscience. To be able to close the barn door to any nuisance of temptation, before it gets to the door, is to preserve the integrity of the interior that was being completely changed.......into a recognizable temple of the Holy Spirit, reflecting God's glory to all who would visit there.

THE WORLD'S GREATEST WATCH DOG

Spike, a big black, shaggy dog, had no pedigree papers, had been abandoned—near the local livestock facility, when my husband found him. He was very timid and any loud noise such as thunder/lightning would chase him under the deck to shake in fear. He needed lots of affection before he would "adopt" us as his family.

Spike never barked much at night. While the coyotes put on their howling performances, he slept on the deck near the patio doors. He walked with me three miles a day during my regular exercise regimen. When I came out the door, he whined and barked—time to go for our walk. God must be as joyful as my dog when I spend time with Him.

Spike and I were both newcomers to this place, when about 30 steers were loose in the yard one morning. I panicked, but Spike stood guard between the house and corral while I covered the other escape route in the front yard. I felt very inadequate but proud of the dog offering his help, with no command from me. I breathed a sigh of relief when they all followed the first one through the gate. Later, it was discovered the animals weren't even ours. We had done a good deed for a neighbor!

One night I heard a playful bark...The porch light revealed a skunk sauntering up the front sidewalk. A few nights later I saw Spike and his striped companion eating dog food together out of the dog pan near the back door.

Spike also shared food with 'possums that were seen walking to and from the back door under the yardlight. One evening, we saw Spike in the pasture playing with yet another of our farm's wild inhabitants, wily coyote. We kept the binoculars by the deck door, but who needed those when wild life was so abundant close to the house? A deer stood watching from the edge of the yard, (during one sleepless night) while Spike "watched" back from his spot on the deck.

I heard a rustling sound in the carport, in the wee hours. When I looked out, there was a large raccoon eating out of the dog food sack while Spike lay near the back of the car, "watching!" He had to be the world's greatest "watch" dog! We had to erect an electric fence to keep the raccoons out of the sweet corn patch that summer.

Lynn Moriarty Parman

Spike gradually got old and stiff and our morning walk would tire him. Obviously, we thought we needed a younger dog to "protect" the farmstead, so we adopted a nine month old Black Lab from the dog pound. Duke was so full of pep that Spike was wary of the "intruder" at first.

Soon Spike was running and playing and miraculously his stiffness had disappeared! He even joined in every time a coyote yapped. I began to miss the nightly coyote "choruses" as Duke carried out his vendetta against cats and wild creatures. Nightly "hunts" were good for Spike; at any rate, he had more energy.

However, Duke's aggressiveness could not be tolerated when he began chasing livestock at night. We gave him away and Spike's energy seemed to leave at the same time. He retired to his post near the deck door. He started to limp, then couldn't move his back legs. The vet said it was tick paralysis. But handicapped as he was, he dragged himself out to the edge of the yard when nature called. He never did that in the yard.

Spike will be remembered for his loyalty on our morning walks, for his non-judgemental attitude toward other critters, for his thoughtful manners (not messing in the yard) and for showing us the importance of exercise for all ages. He certainly was a friend to all.

Surrogate Mother

Our big beautiful Collie had been abandoned by unappreciative townspeople on our gravel road. My husband brought him home and named him "Dawg" after one of John Wayne's movie sidekicks. He was affectionate and gentle and seemed much more cultured than his generic name implied. He shared protective duties with another dog who was old and needed companionship. They chased cats and coyotes together, their fur coats often matted with burrs and ticks.

One cool, summer evening, as the moon was rising in the east, I was bringing in laundry from the clothesline. "Dawg" brought me a present. Tenderly carrying a furry little ball in his mouth, he laid a tiny kitty at my feet. He had heard it crying in the rows of big bales just off the yard, and rescued it. I marveled at this true "Lassie" characteristic that surprisingly showed itself in the farm dog that generally chased every cat. I looked at him with new appreciation.

"Moonbeam" would snuggle in "Dawg's" fur and almost disappear, her yellow coat blending right in. She climbed all over him and he always protected her, would even let her eat with him from his pan. "Moonbeam" was the only cat allowed even close to the house. He licked her with his long tongue, nearly knocking her over. "Grandpa" even became attached to the little orphan, letting her come in the house and keep him company in the evenings, while Dawg jealously stood outside on the deck, whining for attention.

Dawg and Cat would run and play in the yard, real friends. This unusual attachment was only to be enjoyed for a few months. Moonbeam developed a virus that caused convulsions. As I watched, my eyes filled with tears. Dawg was quite perplexed by the strange behavior during her "spells." The Vet informed us that she was a "he." When it was over, we buried her/him down by the big bales where Dawg had originally found her.

So Moonbeam died and the old dog died and "Dawg" was now alone. He seemed depressed as he grieved the loss of his companions. He walked with me when I walked for exercise every morning and he trotted along beside our horses when we rode down along the river. He barked at coyotes and coon, but was now a lone voice in the night. In the winter time Dawg sleeps on the bare ground, sometimes waking up under a blanket of snow. He is a rugged, common old dog, giving his name real significance; and like John Wayne, has a very gentle nature underneath a sometimes gruff exterior.

Lynn Moriarty Parman

TAKING INVENTORY, WHAT'S IN THE FRUIT CELLAR?

How many fruits are stored in the cellar? Would some spoil because I didn't use them soon enough? "There is a time for keeping—a time for throwing away." "A time for planting" and "a time for uprooting what has been planted." Ecc. 3:1-8.

Self-control would be the first fruit that spoiled. Someone else loosened the lid while it was freshly preserved. Once one gets a taste of sexual activity, they can't seem to keep the lid on a desire for selfish pleasure. My mind frequently wandered to sexual thoughts. When I was a child, the recurring nightmare about sex, at an age when I should not have had that kind of knowledge, left questions that had to be answered someday.

The seed of fear, planted in my heart while very young, grew with each episode that left me feeling more rejected. I had to marry because I did not have self-control. If the one fruit was opened too soon, it could spoil other fruits: trustfulness, patience, goodness, peace, joy, and the ability to love (unconditionally).

"There's a time for keeping silent." Is fifty years long enough? "...a time for speaking"—I'm writing it now and it's bringing me peace and more control over my thoughts. I couldn't find the fruit of SELF-CONTROL until I took inventory of what's down there, in the cellar of the unconscious mind. I remember being in another cellar in the dim light when I was about ten, doing my chore of cleaning the milk separator. My brother, hiding in the dark shadows, jumped out, scaring me! I screamed!

I screamed again (a few years ago) when I remembered what was hiding in other, darker memories of childhood. Other survivors are hearing me and together we are "cleaning the cobwebs" out of the fruit cellar. And hiding in the corners, we discover the fruits of the Spirit. I can TRUST because someone believes in me. I find JOY in sharing my insights and helping others, I now have PEACE in my anxious heart, because I "see" how much God loves me. I have more PATIENCE because I know my prayers will be answered, and God knows the best way, for me. He brought me back to the door of the fruit cellar. (Gal. 5:22) (the fruits of the Spirit).

One of my 4-H projects was to preserve three jars that made up a menu. I remember canning beef, sweet corn and fruit. Now I know that Jesus is the "meat," faith is the staple of a healthy spiritual diet and the fruits of the Spirit are my dessert. Without Jesus, I don't have a perfect meal. Jesus said "I am the Way, the Truth and the Life." (JN: 14:6) With Him I have self-control for the temptations of over-indulging in any other area of my life. With God's gift of dessert, I don't need rich foods to "make me feel better."

Lynn Moriarty Parman

The cellar of my soul is no longer cluttered and the SON shines down letting in warmth and drying up any moldy thoughts. These days, PATIENCE is on the front shelf and I've opened the jar of LOVE, learning how to use it "unconditionally." As long as the SON shines in the cellar, any "GOODNESS, KINDNESS and GENTLENESS" will not be hidden in the dark.

We can serve our fruits anywhere we happen to be, and they will not spoil. The flavor will improve as more years pass by. With self-control, we can choose to plant only seeds that we know will reap the best outcome, then expect God to bless that seed and bring it to harvest. When the shelves are stocked with plenty of humility, the cellar will never run out of fruit. "He who abides in me, and I in him, he it is that bears much fruit, for apart from me you can do nothing." (JN. 15:5) RSV

THE THONG TREE

I had seen it several years ago when my husband walked with me along the river banks. It was a thong-tree, the kind that Indians had tied over to point others in the right direction. This day I searched for the tree that was well over 100 years old. I was following deer trails along the river and beginning to perspire. A warm day, (in the 60's), for the end of winter, but a wonderful day for reflections out of doors. "There it is!"

Leaning out over the river with flood debris caught around it's trunk; I had wondered if the great "500 yr flood of '93" had brought about its demise. But there it stood, a monument to the past and those people who prayed to the Spirits for guidance. It pointed to the east—across the river. The only damage was at the end where it had been tied down, (the point) was gone; the point that had curved upwards to the heavens with the passage of time. The old Grand River that had been at least 20 feet away (7 yrs ago) was now eroding away at the root system. With the pile of flood debris, I could not see the natural curve of the bent sapling of a century ago, but every limb had grown straight up out of the horizontal one.

The bank had been cut away by floods and it was probably 15 ft to the surface of the water. I had to find another tree to hang onto while I leaned towards the river to take a picture. The sun was in the wrong place, but I hoped it would work...

I stopped there to rest and write about this lovely late winter morning...The Bible says "Look to the East." When we find the place where God is pointing us, then spring will come. We will begin to grow spiritually and strive to follow the path He directed us to.

At a bend in the river, one bank that used to be lined with trees...is now barren and sandy. We had even seen a 30' Cottonwood floating across the cornfield that devastating summer of the big flood. Who knows where it stopped, miles downstream. That's what may happen to us if we allow our faith to weaken—we may be taken for a ride down the river of circumstances.

It took thousands of steps across a pasture and bean stubble to walk by the river today...it only took a few steps for me to find the right direction several years ago...the 12 steps that helped me put my faith in God.

The dogs see me coming back now across the bean field and start barking...I wave and I can see their tales wag. I'm sure God must be that happy to see me when I look eastward and travel his way.

Lynn Moriarty Parman

Letter From Teddy

My name is Teddy. I came to the farm last March when the weather was about as cold as this November day. Grandpa and Grandma needed a farm dog. Their collie is old and crippled but has become my best friend. His name is "Dawg", named after John Wayne's dog in a movie.

I was an abandoned puppy when I went to the animal shelter. When I was born, I was one of 11 puppies in my mother's litter. She took me down to the pond to drown me. I was scared. I guess she didn't think she could take care of another one. Well, miraculously, I was rescued by a nice lady, (I thought.) She had a dog pen in her back yard so I was protected from stray dogs that might try to hurt me. But the lady left town one day and never came back. I was hungry and cried for days.

Once again I was rescued, this time by the police because the lady was charged with cruelty to animals. They took me to the animal shelter where I was confined to a much smaller cage. It made me so sad. Many kids came to find a pet, but I couldn't be adopted because they couldn't find the owner to give permission for my adoption. I barked a lot, wanting out of that cage. A lot of people came to look at all the dogs in the cages.

They thought I was weird! I do look strange with short legs and big feet, like a Bassett; my reddish tipped black coat and curled tail from a Chow grandparent and my face which looks like a Black Lab ancestor. I really am a mixture.

One day the middle-aged farm couple came to the shelter looking for a young companion for their collie. I was 9 mo. old and the farm-wife loved me from the moment she saw me. I had been in the shelter for four months. I was very friendly and she liked my thick coat (like a Teddy bear).

They took me home that day and I love the farm. They wanted a dog to protect the place from intruders. I found out what kind of intruders they get in the country! The coyotes howl all night long and come up close to the buildings to tease the dogs. Then raccoons sneak into the machine shed at night and climb up on the combine.

Dawg and I decided on a strategy hiding in the shadows. We chased one up a tree by the bathroom window and he slept there most of the next day. We have to be careful because some of the wild animals have rabies. The farmer decided I needed a rabies vaccination if I was going to be doing hand-to-hand combat with wild animals.

Raccoons look cute up a tree but can be vicious fighters. During one of our encounters, Dawg got a patch of fur torn off his side, skin and all. It took all summer to heal with Grandma spraying something on it. We've had our noses scratched up, leaving scars there too.

I seldom bark here at my new home. We chase cats and most anything else that walks on four legs, but I can't chase the cattle or they tie me up. That's the only time I bark—when I am confined. Guess it reminds me of my past, then I am protesting.

I got in trouble last week when they were running cattle across the road into the corral. I came out from under a pickup and chased them (only they went six directions instead of through the right gate.) Grandpa was really angry at me and Grandma tied me up until they got the critters all in the corral. Some of them took off running down the road and Grandpa hopped in a vehicle to go after them and herd them back up to the yard. They got put in the corral until they were all ready to be hauled to the sale barn.

Cold weather is already here. Grandpa has been cutting firewood and made a doghouse out of straw in the shed near the barn. It's been below freezing the last two nights.

I'm a pretty good dog. I Never pull things off the clothesline or dig holes by the house. Dawg does that and Grandma gets real upset when her flower beds are disturbed.

Mitchell came to play with me one day. He's 8 and we had so much fun. When will you come to the farm to see me? Hope it's real soon!

Teddy

ONE LEG UP

Someone once said that "one leg up" meant having an advantage over somebody. Just being able to stand on my legs and walk is a gift. I walk for my Mom and many others who cannot get out and do so. One leg up brings to mind lifting a leg to climb the stairs. Sometimes that can be painful, but oh how those who can't even do that fondly wish that they could.

When I think of one leg up I also think about the dog desecrating the flower beds or bushes in the yard. That is a bad habit to try to break them of and may eventually kill some plants. I pray that I will cultivate good habits so that no one will be harmed by what I do.

My country road has been a great inspiration for me to get out and raise my legs. The more I walk the better I feel. I remember when I was recovering from vein surgery. Both legs felt like cement posts—there had been 56 incisions. My husband said "Your legs look like you have been *fighting tigers*. Well, it felt like it too! But I began walking a few feet more each day until I was able to go a whole two miles.

I watched a centipede about two inches long crawl across the road. He has so many pairs of legs to assist his walk, surely he would not miss a couple if he were injured? I have only two, none to fall back on. It had no trouble climbing in the grass with so many legs to give himself a boost. I have to lift all of me with each step on one leg. That thought alone ought to be enough to motivate me to lose a few pounds.

I often go far enough to walk over the little wooden bridge down the road…walking in itself is a bridge to better health. A stalk of Mullein with its bright yellow blooms stands like a sentinel along the road. Mullein is known in holistic medicine as having medicinal properties. Walking is my sentinel. It may help me to stand taller for a little while longer and that is one leg up on those who don't choose to exercise!

Lynn Moriarty Parman

MUSHROOM MARATHON

Toting a gallon bucket with handle, we charged off into the pasture next to an old cemetery as we set out on our quest. First time ever for me to "hunt" mushrooms. Would I have to stand on my head to see through my bi-focals when I wasn't sure what a Morel even looked like?

Mushroom hunting doesn't take much preparation compared to other sports. No guns or protective gear. There's no need for special permits or identifiable colors on your person either. You just need reliable transportation to the area that you think might be bountiful. The Midwest is particularly blessed with the right combination of favorable factors.

Late April or early May is a great time to walk through the woods anyway before the underbrush begins to grow. An appreciation for the out-of-doors and nature's habitat is a bonus, but certainly not required. The woods seem to be alive with wildflowers such as Trillium, Columbine, and Orchids. Violets, Phlox and Bloodroot sprinkled everywhere and Umbrella plants with large delicate rounded leaves and milky green stems take on the aura of a story-book forest.

Now you are set for an adventure that will have you coming back again and again. The need to "conquer" will spur you on to new pastures before the season ends, which can happen as suddenly as it began. No date on the calendar—a warm balmy spring breeze and gentle rain combine to set off the Morel's sensitive alarm clock, which might be anytime of the day or night.

The bugle call goes out to the neighborhood, "I found a mushroom!" Then anyone who's ever observed this woodsy ritual, is off to his favorite "haunt," and NOBODY is telling where they found one!

The "No Hunting" and "No Trespassing" warnings posted on local fences and gates seem to go unnoticed during this traditional seasonal phenomenon. The "hunt is on" and the community sets out to see who can find the biggest Morel of the year. And the local newspaper awaits the results with the same anticipation as recording the biggest set of deer antlers.

Our chosen destination was heavily inundated with Multiflora Rose and Gooseberry thickets. We pushed through, arms thrust overhead, crossing a small stream several times as it wandered through a maze of trees. My sixty-year old adventurous husband-guide, had more stamina than a young athlete, his long limbs taking half as many strides as mine. When we'd cross a fence, he'd hold up one wire and step on another while I crawled through. But I ripped my finger on a barbed wire, in spite of his helpfulness.

No animals visable, though deer tracks were plentiful and last year's squirrel nests held fast, high up in the treetops. My clever leader said,

"They probably heard us coming a mile away," as we crashed through the heavy carpet of last year's fallen leaves that blanketed the floor of the woods. A cunning, research-type personality might be helpful. No problem there, I fit that category—invariably having to "find" lost articles. I just poked underneath the leaves, looking for the elusive treasure.

After a recent rain, the ravine bottoms were damp and streams ran full, a beautiful sight following two drought years in a row. I scouted for a narrow crossing to accomodate my short pair of limbs, fearful I would be left behind.

However, one fleeting moment of childhood courage propelled my body halfway up a dead log that leaned on a ten-foot embankment on the opposite side of the creek. With sure-footed tennies, I thought it would be a breeze! But there I was, bucket in hand, legs froze, like a fox with no tail to balance myself. I could not pick up either foot!

Throwing the bucket ahead, to the far side, I tried (unsuccessfully) to bend down and touch the log to steady the fear that was racing through every cell of my aging body. *"What was I going to do if the log shifted?"* One limb that it rested on was decayed, a fact that I failed to notice, when I leaped impulsively onto that native bridge. My veteran tracker was out of sight behind the bank, having crossed safely atop his lanky ladderlegs.

I pictured myself inching the remaining six or seven feet by straddling the plank. *"But what about those knees that seem hopelessly locked in position?"* I thought. Eventually, the old torso did bend in the middle allowing me to grasp the bark, like a stiff-armed octopus, to pull myself, hands and feet, very slowly to the high side of that precarious perch. Confident Guide showed up just in time to pull me the last two frightening feet. Looking over the conditions of the log, he chastised me with these words,

"What if you fell and broke a leg? How would I ever get you out of there?"

By then, my guide wasn't sure exactly where we were. We had made a complete circle, winding up in the same spot we knew we had been before, where someone long ago had left what appeared to be a deer blind above our heads in a tree. He knew the whole county, just wasn't familiar with this one square mile of brushy timber. No matter—I trusted him, even if I did get slapped in the face by a branch for following too closely.

We approached a clearing on top of a hill, where we could pick out some local landmarks—a rural water tower and a couple of farm buildings. Now my legs ached clear to my waist with every uphill thrust. I definitely seemed to lack the endurance of a first class marathon runner even though I thought I was in pretty good physical shape when I began this little outing. My guide had told me what to look for specifically, as I contemplated whether any mushrooms grew here at all! Maybe it was just a fable?

Halfway up the next hill, a huge log over the trail beckoned like a long rustic bench; and we made use of it. There was a wonderful hush in the air as the wind swirled through the high tips of the trees. The air had cooled off several degrees, so I kept my hands in my pockets while bending over our bench, hoping to see a mushroom. But they were 100% successful at avoiding us. I felt humbled, like we had passed hundreds of them, shaking with laughter because they had outwitted us.

I could hear my heart quiet down as the whisper of bygone days settled around us. We could envision Indians hunting nearby. A deer carcass lay sprawled at the edge of a clearing—the victim of a hunting season past. Coyotes had savored a gourmet meal.

With renewed vigor, the quest continued. "Look," I shouted. I had always dreamed of a place in the woods, by a lake. Here was the perfect hideaway (an A-frame cottage) in the middle of an open space on the hill overlooking a placid pond. What a retreat! It made brambles and barbed wire seem utterly insignificant.

As we trudged up yet another hill, our pace quickened. Approaching the dwelling, cautiously, we wondered what they would think about us coming out of the woods like that? Fearless Guide said,

"We'll probably be arrested."

"Well, then we would get a ride,"

I ventured, doubtful whether those lower limbs could even complete another trek through the woods, that particular day.

All was vacant, but the fenced-in yard had been mowed. A neatly stacked wood pile and outdoor grill were ready for summer. Spying an outhouse, I investigated out of pure biological need, taking advantage of a bit more modern convenience in the raw pioneer setting.

It seemed that our pickup was less than a mile away. On the journey back, my mind lingered in fantasyland. The edible morsels were still asleep and my very first "Morel" had turned out to be someone else's delicacy.

The sight of that cozy cabin in the woods brought me as much joy as thinking about 1Cor 2:9. "no mere man has ever seen, heard or imagined what wonderful things God has ready for those who love the Lord." (LB) At the end of this whole life marathon will be the mansions too wonderful for words and my woodsy cabin dream would pale by comparison. "Run then in such a way as to win the prize...but...do it for one that will last forever." 1 Cor 9:24-26 Good News for Modern Man

Printed in the United States
23344LVS00002B/341-350